IS IT GOD'S WILL TO HEAL *You?*

JULENE HODGES SCHROEDER

IS IT GOD'S WILL TO HEAL
Your?

JULENE HODGES SCHROEDER

Summer Bay Press

Is It God's Will to Heal YOU?

Copyright © 2018 Julene Hodges Schroeder

Published by Summer Bay Press
Cover design, interior design: Wendy Dewar Hughes, Summer Bay
Press
Editing: Carolee Hodges Harbour

ISBN: 978-1-927626-83-2
Digital ISBN: 978-1-927626-84-9

Library and Archives Canada Cataloguing in Publication
Schroeder, Julene Hodges, 1951—

All *italicized emphases* are the author's.

CONTENTS

INTRODUCTION

Is It God's Will To Heal YOU?

Some time ago, I was talking to a friend who has lived a life of pain, and suffered from one ailment after another. She had patiently listened to the messages on healing and read the articles I'd sent her, but I could tell she did not believe it was always God's will to heal everybody.

As we stood there and talked briefly, I thought to myself, *If I could just come home with you for a week, with nothing but my Bible, I'm sure I could help you see that it is always God's will to heal everybody and it is especially His will for you to be healed completely.*

You might think that is an outrageous statement, considering the number of people you know, perhaps even yourself, who have prayed to be healed and yet not felt any differently afterward.

But let's say I am privileged to spend a few days with you and share what I have studied in my Bible for the past forty years. Starting at the beginning, and going through to the end of the Bible, I would explain why it has convinced me it is always God's will to heal you and me, even when circumstances seem to say otherwise.

THE LAW OF FIRST MENTION

Let's go back to the beginning. Theologians speak of the "Law of First Mention," which states that the first time a subject is mentioned in the Bible, it sets God's standard for that subject throughout the Bible. Most of these "first mentions" are in the book of Genesis, naturally, because it is the book of beginnings.

For instance, take a beautiful topic like love. What would God say about love the very first time it is mentioned? The word first appears in Genesis 22:2:

> Then [God] said [to Abraham], "Take now
> your son, your only son Isaac, whom you *love*
> and go...offer him there as a burnt offering."

In that first mention of "love," God set His standard. Abraham did not actually have to kill his son, because God stopped him, but God was showing what love was, for a few centuries later, God gave His Son, His only Son, whom He loved, to die – and the sacrifice was for all mankind, for God *so loved* the world (John 3:16).

When was "healing" first mentioned?

In Genesis 20:17 it says: "So Abraham prayed to God; and God healed..."

The first time healing is ever mentioned, right from the beginning of the Bible, God showed us that when prayer is made for healing, He heals.

1

GOD'S COVENANT NAME AS HEALER

God revealed Himself to His people in the Old Testament by names which were prefaced by "Jehovah." Each name showed a different, unchanging characteristic about God that He wanted to reveal to His people. By the time He had revealed the final one in the last verse of Ezekiel, the Israelites had a beautiful picture of their wonderful God.

When the Children of Israel first came out of Egypt, we are told that "there was none feeble among their tribes" (Psalm 105:37). Some versions say "there was no one sick among their tribes." Although there would have been many old people with infirmities, and many who had been cruelly treated as slaves all their lives or who had injuries or sicknesses, when they left Egypt they all experienced healing. Out of over 600,000 fighting men, plus all the other men, women and children, no one was limping, there were no stretchers, no weak people, none sick. Everyone was healed.

After they had crossed the Red Sea, when they met their first major obstacle (bitter water), God spoke to them. He showed Moses a tree (symbolic of the cross), which Moses threw into the water, which then became sweet. God then revealed a new covenant name to them. Exodus 15:25-26 tells us:

> There He tested them, and there He made a
> statute and an ordinance for them and said, "If
> you diligently heed the voice of the Lord your

God and do what is right in His sight, give ear to His commandments and keep all His statutes, I will [allow]ⁱ none of the diseases on you which I have [allowed] on the Egyptians, for I am the Lord who heals you."

Today, as New Testament believers, we don't have to keep rules and laws in order to earn God's healing. Jesus completely wiped out all those commandments, statutes and ordinances and nailed them to His cross (Colossians 2:14), leaving us with the new commandment to love one another (John 13:34). God is still the Lord that heals us, but today we receive it because *Jesus* perfectly kept and fulfilled the whole law for us.

Most importantly, Exodus 15:26 gives us God's covenant name: "the Lord who heals you." With this name, God reveals an extremely significant aspect of His unchanging character.

THE BRONZE SERPENT

After the Israelites had travelled in the wilderness for quite a while, they came to the border of Edom, but Edom refused to allow them to travel through their land (Numbers 21). Moses had to lead the people around the land of Edom.

Go around? The desert had already been endless! They were fed up with it and having nothing but manna to eat every day. They began to complain bitterly, declaring it would even be better to die than go on. They threatened to overthrow Moses and appoint a leader to take them back to Egypt.

Suddenly snakes began to appear among the complainers, biting and killing people. The people's tone changed quickly and they ran to Moses, asking him to pray to God for them. Numbers 21:7-9 says:

> So Moses prayed for the people. Then the Lord said to Moses, "Make a fiery serpent, and set it on a pole; and it shall be that everyone who is bitten, when he looks at it, shall live."
> So Moses made a bronze serpent, and put it on a pole; and so it was, if a serpent had bitten anyone, when he looked at the bronze serpent, he lived.

Notice God said *everyone* who looked at it would live. Absolutely *anyone* who was bitten was healed if he looked at the serpent.

Jesus said in John 3:14-15 that this story foretold His being "lifted up" on a cross for the world. The serpent on the pole was the "type" or foreshadowing of Jesus. Jesus was the fulfillment or "antitype." If *anyone* was healed by looking at the bronze serpent, would not *everyone* who looks in faith to Jesus, the antitype, also live and be healed today?

THE CURSE OF THE LAW

Because the Israelites, like any human beings, were incapable of keeping such a vast amount of laws, God gave them incentives and punishments. The incentives were blessings which, to be frank, are mind-boggling. The punishments were dire consequences, called curses, which would eventually come on them if they refused to obey.

Deuteronomy 28 spells out these blessings and curses more clearly than any other passage. The first fourteen verses tell of unimaginable blessings that God promised to pour out on His people if they obeyed His law. The rest of the chapter lists one terrible curse after another, including many sicknesses, for disobeying the law. Finally, in verse 61, God says:

> Also every sickness and every plague, which is not written in this Book of the Law, will the Lord [allow to come]ⁱⁱ upon you until you are destroyed.

Notice God was saying in this chapter that He considered *every* sickness and *every* plague a curse. Have you considered that every little (or serious) sickness you have had to endure is a curse? The Bible indicates it is.

But here is the best news: we are redeemed from *all* those curses! Galatians 3:13 says:

> Christ has redeemed us from the curse of the law, having become a curse for us (for it is

written, "Cursed is everyone who hangs on a tree").

Anything Jesus redeemed us from, we do not have to endure. He destroyed its power and gave us authority over it (Luke 10:19).

A KING WHO DIDN'T PRAY FOR HEALING

Asa was a godly king in the Old Testament who caused his people to turn back to God. Not too long after he had instituted major reforms, a huge army of a million men with hundreds of chariots came against him. Israel's troops would have been like a small, poorly-equipped army today trying to fight off forces ten times its size, which had state-of-the-art warplanes, tanks and missiles.

Asa recognized his only hope and cried out to the Lord (2 Chronicles 14:11) and God gave a great and miraculous victory to the Israelites.

In the next chapter, Asa, was faced with a much smaller army. Instead of crying out to God as he had the first time, he took things into his own hands and made a deal with a king nearby to help him. God was not impressed. "Were the Ethiopians and the Lubim not a huge army with very many chariots and horsemen?" He asked. "Yet because you relied on the Lord, He delivered them into your hand." Then He said those famous words: "For the eyes of the Lord run to and fro throughout the whole earth, to show Himself strong on behalf of those whose heart is loyal to Him."

Asa did not rely on God one more time and this time it cost him his life. 2 Chronicles 16:12-13 reads:

> And in the thirty-ninth year of his reign, Asa
> became diseased in his feet, and his malady

was severe; yet in his disease he did not seek
the Lord, but the physicians. So Asa [died].

There are many of God's people today, unfortunately, of whom the same thing could be said. When they are sick, it doesn't occur to them to seek the Lord, but only the physicians. (Some even state they believe it is not God's will to heal them, but at the same time they are actively seeking natural, medical healing.) Why would God record that story? He did because from the beginning of the Bible, He had proven He wanted to be His people's healer, cure their diseases and answer all their prayers for healing. He loves to show Himself strong to those whose hearts are loyal to *Him*, who do not look to others for help first and to Him only as a last resort.

Going to the doctor or taking medicine is not a sin. God created the herbs and chemicals used for medicine that heal our bodies and He has given amazing skills to medical personnel. But let us not be like Asa, and put our full trust in those things instead of seeking God, who had already shown Himself so strong to Asa when he sought him for a miracle.

TWO BEAUTIFUL PSALMS

Psalm 103 is such a favourite of mine. The words are tender, so affectionate. I read the verses over and over and am always touched by them. Verses 2 and 3 say:

Bless the Lord, O my soul, and forget not all
His benefits; who forgives all your iniquities,
who heals all your diseases.

For years I confidently believed the first benefit — that God forgives all my iniquities — but balked over the second, "heals all your diseases." It seemed like God couldn't mean that. Not from what I'd observed. Nevertheless, God said it was a benefit He never wants us to forget. He said He heals all of our diseases as surely as He forgives all our sins when we ask.

Then Psalm 107:19-21 tells of people becoming ill, again as a curse for disobeying the law:

Fools, because of their transgression, and because of their iniquities, were afflicted. Their soul abhorred all manner of food, and they drew near to the gates of death. Then they cried out to the Lord in their trouble, and He saved them out of their distresses. *He sent His word and healed them,* and delivered them from their destructions. Oh, that men would give thanks to the Lord for His goodness, and for His wonderful works to the children of men!

First of all, note that these people were called "fools." In their case, they were foolish because of sins and transgressions. They experienced the curse of sickness for turning away from God and His law. But when they cried out to the Lord, in His great goodness, He sent His word and healed them, even though they didn't deserve it.

In our case, let's look at foolishness in a different way. Have you ever been foolish, and stayed up late too many nights, eaten too much junk food, or done something careless which made you hurt yourself?

Has your body ever stomped its feet and said, "OK, this time I'm not going to try to heal you"? No, our bodies were programmed *by God* as part of the natural process to do their very best to heal us every single time we get sick. Never does the body ask how we got sick, how many sins we committed, or if we were foolish. God programmed His instructions into humans' immune systems from the very beginning: heal!

The same is true in the supernatural realm. No matter how foolish or sinful we have been, when we cry out to God for healing, He sends His word and heals us (Psalm 107:20).

"His word" could be interpreted as His written Word, which He said is health and medicine to all our flesh (Proverbs 4:22). "His word" could mean His command. Or it could represent Jesus (John 1:1), the Word whom God sent to bear all our sicknesses and take them away from us (Matthew 8:17).

THE GREAT EXCHANGE

Now we come to the greatest verses on healing in the whole Bible. Three places say the same thing: once in the Old Testament, once during Jesus' ministry, and once near the end of the Bible. These are the verses which tell what Jesus did for us on the cross, enduring our penalty and setting us free from all the works of the devil. First, Isaiah 53:4-5 says:

> Surely He has borne our griefs and carried our sorrows; yet we esteemed Him stricken, smitten by God and afflicted. But He was wounded for our transgressions, He was bruised for our iniquities; the chastisement for our peace was upon Him, and by His stripes we are healed.

If you have ever lost a loved one or experienced grief and sorrow, you know how very supernaturally real God's comfort is, especially when others are praying for you. But the words "griefs" and "sorrows" are translated in many versions as "sicknesses" and "pains."

Also, "peace" in Isaiah 53:5 is the all-encompassing and wonderful Hebrew word "shalom," which means "wholeness, peace, health, safety, well-being, prosperity, rest, harmony, favour, tranquility, completeness, contentment"[iii] The chastisement for all those blessings was laid on Jesus so we could experience them.

Secondly, we come to the story in the New Testament where Jesus healed every single person who came to Him in order to fulfill the above verses. Matthew 8:16-17 says:

> When evening had come, they brought to Him many who were demon-possessed. And He cast out the spirits with a word, and healed all who were sick, that it might be fulfilled which was spoken by Isaiah the prophet, saying, "He Himself took our infirmities and bore our sicknesses."

When Jesus died, He paid the price for every sin that had been committed or would ever be committed. Can you imagine a person asking God to forgive him, and God saying, "Oh, no, Jesus didn't bear *that* sin"?

In the same substitutionary death, the Bible says Jesus bore every sickness, every infirmity and every disease. It should be hard to imagine that a person could ask God to heal a disease, and God saying, "Oh, no, Jesus didn't take *that* sickness. I'm sorry, you will have to bear that one yourself"?

Worst of all, can you imagine believing that the "Lord who heals us" *put* a sickness on us?

No, a thousand times, no! Jesus paid the price for every sin, every trespass, every mistake committed on the earth. At the same time, He bore every sickness, every weakness, every pain, every wretched disease and plague. Not one was left out. The entire curse of sickness that came on the world when Adam sinned ("and death came upon all men" — Romans 5:12), was laid on Jesus. He took the punishment and paid the penalty for it all.

Thirdly, at the end of the Bible, 1 Peter 2:24 tells us what happened when Jesus died:

> Who Himself bore our sins in His own body on the tree, that we, having died to sins, might

live for righteousness — by whose stripes you were healed.

This time healing is in the past tense — *"you were healed."* Jesus had already died and risen from the dead. When He died, He took our sicknesses. You and I were actually healed 2000 years ago.

THE GREATEST REVELATION ON HEALING

We *were* healed! That is the greatest revelation we can ever receive in regard to healing. In reality, we are not *the sick* who have to come to God to beg for healing. The actual fact is that you and I *were* healed and just need to know how to stand against our deadly enemy, the devil, who is forever trying to steal our purchased, completed healing from us.

It does take a change in thinking, but it is possible. When our minds are renewed to this life-transforming truth, we will look at sickness very differently. Instead of seeing ourselves as helpless victims of it, we will realize we are redeemed from sickness and God has given us authority over it. Legally it cannot stay if we refuse to allow it.

The natural mind says, "I feel sick, I look sick, the doctor says I'm sick; therefore, I am sick."

The renewed mind says, "I feel sick, I look sick, the doctor says I'm sick, but there is a truth which supersedes all that — Jesus took this sickness and God says, *'By His stripes I am healed.'*"

Forever Settled

Psalm 119:89 says that God's Word is forever settled in heaven. If it were possible to ask anyone in heaven if you are healed — friends, relatives, angels, or God Himself — they would respond to you, "Yes, you are healed by Jesus' stripes. That fact is forever settled here."

15

We just have to come to believe that truth and enforce it in our lives, so that it becomes a reality in the natural realm as well as the spiritual realm.

Are you beginning to get a glimpse of how our thinking must change if we are going to walk in the health that Jesus died to give us and operate in the authority He gave us over the works of the devil? As you meditate on all that is involved in Jesus' priceless gift, your thought patterns will begin to become transformed until you are convinced of these infallible truths.

HEALING IN THE MINISTRY OF JESUS

Hebrews 10:7 tells us that when Jesus came to earth, He said, "I have to come...to do Your will, O God." Because of that, we can accept that everything recorded about Jesus' life was God's will. Every time He cast out a demon, healed a sick person, or did a miracle, He did it because God had instructed Him to.

With that in mind, let's look at what the gospels say about Jesus' ministry *(emphases mine).*

Matthew 9:35:

Then Jesus went about all the cities and villages, teaching in their synagogues, preaching the gospel of the kingdom, and *healing every sickness and every disease* among the people.

Matthew 12:15

But when Jesus knew it, He withdrew from there. And great multitudes followed Him, and *He healed them all.*

Mark 6:56

Wherever He entered, into villages, cities or the country, they laid the sick in the market places, and begged Him that they might just

17

touch the hem of His garment. And *as many as touched Him were made well.*

Luke 4:40
When the sun was setting, all those who had any that were sick with various diseases brought them to Him; and *He laid His hands on every one of them and healed them.*

Luke 6:19
And the whole multitude sought to touch Him, for power went out from Him and *healed them all.*

Luke 9:11
But when the multitudes knew it, they followed Him; and He received them and spoke to them about the kingdom of God, and *healed those who had need of healing.*

What stands out in the gospels is the complete absence of any case where a person came to Jesus for healing and Jesus telling that person it was not God's will for him or her to be healed.

No, Jesus never turned anyone away with those words. He never refused to heal one person in all the gospels, because He had come to do His Father's will. And it was God's will that all be healed.

There was, however, one man who did wonder if it was God's will. He knew Jesus *could* heal him, but did not know if He was *willing.* That man was a leper.

Few people on earth were more outcast or despised than lepers. When they discovered they had leprosy, they had to leave their homes, their loved ones and everything dear. If they were forced to be among people, they had to cry, "Unclean!" and people would flee from them. Imagine how despised and rejected they would begin to feel after a short while.

Maybe this man thought that Jesus would reject him too.

But in Matthew 8:2-3, we read:

> Behold, a leper came and worshiped Him, saying, "Lord, if You are willing, You can make me clean." Then Jesus put out His hand and touched him, saying, "*I am willing*; be cleansed." Immediately his leprosy was cleansed.

Jesus, demonstrating the infinite love and compassion of God, reached out and touched this poor outcast, so starved for human touch, then told him how willing He was to heal him. The only person on record who asked if it was God's will, instantly found out — it is always God's will to heal everybody.

WHERE DOES SICKNESS COME FROM?

In Acts 10:38, we see the most perfect summary of Jesus' ministry:

> God anointed Jesus of Nazareth with the Holy
> Spirit and with power, who went about doing
> good and healing all who were oppressed of
> the devil, for God was with Him.

This verse says several important things:

- The reason God anointed Jesus was to "heal all."
- When Jesus healed all, God says He was "doing good."
- All the sick whom Jesus healed were "oppressed by the devil."
- God was "with Him" when Jesus healed all, because Jesus was carrying out God's will.

Today we can stand against every single sickness, knowing they are all from the devil.

1 John 3:8 tells us that "for this purpose the Son of God was manifested, that He might destroy the works of the devil." Other scriptures also indicate that sickness is from the devil:

> Luke 13:16: Jesus said, "Ought not this
> woman, being a daughter of Abraham, *whom*
> *Satan has bound*—think of it—for eighteen
> years, be loosed from this bond on the
> Sabbath?"

John 10:10: Jesus also said, "*The thief* does not come except to steal, and to kill, and to destroy. I have come that they may have life, and that they may have it more abundantly."

Ephesians 6:12: "We do not wrestle against flesh and blood, but against principalities, against powers, against the rulers of the darkness of this age, against spiritual hosts of wickedness in the heavenly places."

These scriptures clearly state where sickness comes from. Sickness was one of the works of the devil in 1 John 3:8 that the Son of God destroyed when He died and rose from the dead.

If Jesus came to one of our cities today to hold a healing meeting, how many sick people do you think He would heal? He would heal every person that came to Him and every disease, because that is God's will. How do I know? I know because this most wonderful verse of all tells me:

Jesus Christ is the same yesterday, today and forever.

Hebrews 13:8

Some scholars believe that only in certain periods in history did God heal people and He seldom heals today. But Hebrews 13:8 says He never changes. Therefore:

- Since God healed "anyone" and "everyone" in the Old Testament who looked to the bronze serpent, a type of Christ,
- Since Jesus "healed all" who came to Him when He walked the earth,
- Since He "healed all" several times through His disciples in the book of Acts,
- And since He is the same yesterday, today and forever,

then please believe me, my friend: He still wants to "heal all" who come to Him today for healing. He wants to heal you!

BUT I HAVE QUESTIONS

Let's start dealing with some questions. I myself have had hands laid on me in the name of Jesus, in accordance with Mark 16:17-18, and felt no better afterwards. You probably have too, which may be why you have believed it was not always God's will to heal you. Even the disciples once had trouble with healing. Matthew 17:14-20 says:

> When they had come to the multitude, a man came to Him, kneeling down to Him and saying, "Lord, have mercy on my son, for he is an epileptic and suffers severely; for he often falls into the fire and often into the water. So I brought him to Your disciples, but they could not cure him."
>
> Then Jesus answered and said, "O faithless and perverse generation, how long shall I be with you? How long shall I bear with you? Bring him here to Me." And Jesus rebuked the demon, and it came out of him; and the child was cured from that very hour.
>
> Then the disciples came to Jesus privately and said, "Why could not we cast it out?" So Jesus said to them, "Because of your unbelief."

If you and I had been there when the disciples prayed for the boy, and saw he wasn't cured, we could have said, "I guess it wasn't God's will for him to be healed, or he would have been healed when the disciples prayed for him." But, wait! When Jesus came on the scene, He showed us what God's will really was. He healed the boy when the disciples couldn't.

His disciples did not know why they had been unable to cast out the devil and heal the boy. Jesus had sent these same disciples on missions before and they had cured many people, cast out devils and done amazing miracles. But this time they couldn't. Why not? Jesus said this time it was because of their unbelief.

Many people today have the same question. They know they have faith. Why isn't it working, then? The problem the disciples had to contend with, and the thing that steals our healing over and over again is dealing with the doubts that the devil (called "the thief" in John 10:10) bombards our minds with when we are believing. These doubts always try to rob us of our answers. In this case, the disciples were kept from success, because the unbelief that was assailing them was too great.

Although, when you think of it, who could not benefit from having more faith? I have not yet multiplied food and fed thousands. I have not walked on water. I have been afraid when my life was threatened. Jesus told His disciples in those cases that they had "no faith" or "little faith" and He was not insulting them. He was stating a fact. A fact which could be changed. It was changed, too, for Acts 5:15-16 says:

> They brought the sick out into the streets and
> laid them on beds and couches, that at least
> the shadow of Peter passing by might fall on
> some of them. Also a multitude gathered from
> the surrounding cities to Jerusalem, bringing
> sick people and those who were tormented by
> unclean spirits, and *they were all healed.*

This verse shows us that the disciples did something about that unbelief. It did not hold them back as it had before.

Another Case Where Unbelief Prevented Healing

There was even a time when Jesus wanted to heal people, but they had too much unbelief and He couldn't because of their unbelief. Mark 6:1-6 says:

> Then [Jesus] went from there and came to His own country, and His disciples followed Him. And when the Sabbath had come, He began to teach in the synagogue. And many hearing Him were astonished, saying, "Where did this Man get these things? And what wisdom is this which is given to Him, that such mighty works are performed by His hands! Is not this the carpenter, the Son of Mary, and brother of James, Joses, Judas, and Simon? And are not His sisters here with us?" So they were offended at Him...
> Now He could do no mighty work there, except that He laid His hands on a few sick people and healed them. And *He marveled because of their unbelief.*

It is interesting that verse 5 does not say Jesus "*would* do no mighty work"; it said "he *could* do no mighty work." The unbelief of the people in His hometown prevented Jesus from healing them.

Our unbelief also prevents Him. This does not mean that God is angry with us or that we are not deeply loved. It simply means every believer on earth will always have to fight against unbelief. God is not unfair. He tells us we must have faith to please Him and receive answers to prayer (Hebrews 11:6), but He also tells us how "faith comes" — by hearing the Word (Romans 10:17).

OTHER ASSURANCES OF HEALING

In Mark 16, Jesus gave His disciples the commission to go into all the world and preach "the gospel" to every creature. They knew that "the gospel" included healing, because they had walked with and watched Jesus for three years. Jesus said in Mark 16:17-18:

> And these signs will follow those who believe:
> In My name they will cast out demons; they
> will speak with new tongues; they will take up
> serpents; and if they drink anything deadly, it
> will by no means hurt them; they will lay
> hands on the sick, and they will recover.

The unfortunate thing is that the above signs do not follow all believers, because not all believers believe in them. But those who do believe and tell this good news to the world, do see those signs.

The disciples took Jesus at His word and Jesus did what He said He would do. One good example is when Paul and Barnabas were preaching the gospel in Lystra. Look what happened in Acts 14:8-10:

> And in Lystra a certain man without strength
> in his feet was sitting, a cripple from his
> mother's womb, who had never walked. This
> man heard Paul speaking. Paul, observing him
> intently and seeing that he had faith to be
> healed, said with a loud voice, "Stand up

straight on your feet!" And he leaped and walked.

If Paul had been preaching that Jesus wanted to forgive people's sins, but it was not always His will for everyone to be healed, would this man have had faith to be healed? No. But Paul was preaching "the gospel," which included healing, for as the man *heard* him speak, *faith came* into his heart for healing. Paul, seeing it, stopped the whole meeting and told him to stand up with those legs and feet that never had walked in his whole life. The man did! He was completely healed.

Let me say here that if you believe it is not always God's will to heal everyone, the next time you are attacked with sickness, the devil will tell you it is not God's will to heal *you*. But if you know it is always God's will to heal everyone, you can fight off that lie and receive the healing that is yours.

IS *ANYONE* SICK?

James 5:14-15 says:

> Is anyone among you sick? Let him call for the
> elders of the church, and let them pray over
> him, anointing him with oil in the name of the
> Lord. And the prayer of faith will save the sick,
> and the Lord will raise him up.

If James knew that it was not God's will to heal everyone, he would not have said, "Is *anyone* sick?" for those words open it up for everyone. But what thrills me is that he is unequivocal in stating they will be healed. The only prerequisite is that the prayer which is offered be "the prayer of faith."

He goes on to say in verse 16:

> Confess your trespasses to one another, and pray
> for one another that you may be healed. The
> effective, fervent prayer of a righteous man avails
> much.

Again, he affirms that the reason for praying for one another is "that you may be healed," not "perhaps you will be healed," or "you might not."

Do you notice in all the verses we have studied, from the book of Genesis to the book of James, this truth is completely consistent? Whether the Bible is telling us that *anyone* who looks at the bronze serpent will be healed, or that God's name is "the Lord who heals us," or that "by His stripes we are healed" in

29

Isaiah to "by His stripes you were healed" in 1 Peter, to the many times Jesus "healed them all," to the book of James where it says, "Is *anyone* sick?" the theme is always the same. We are given unqualified confidence in every case that God will heal.

WHAT ABOUT PAUL'S THORN?

Probably more than any other reason, people believe the story of Paul's thorn proves God does not always want to heal. Let us look closely at 2 Corinthians 12:7-10:

> Lest I should be exalted above measure by the abundance of the revelations, a thorn in the flesh was given to me, a messenger of Satan to buffet me, lest I be exalted above measure. Concerning this thing I pleaded with the Lord three times that it might depart from me. And He said to me, "My grace is sufficient for you, for My strength is made perfect in weakness." Therefore most gladly I will rather boast in my infirmities, that the power of Christ may rest upon me.

I think the reason people believe this is sickness is because of the word "infirmities." The word "infirmities" is used at times in scripture to mean sickness. But it is also used to speak of "weakness, lack of strength, lack of capacity needed to understand a thing"[iv] in these verses:

> Romans 8:26 says the Holy Spirit helps our infirmities because we don't know how to pray as we ought.

Romans 15:1 says we ought to bear the infirmities of the weak and not just to please ourselves.

Hebrews 4:15 tells us that we have a High Priest who sympathizes with our weaknesses, which in the Greek is the same word as "infirmities."

So, let's look at this passage with that in mind. In 2 Corinthians 12:5, Paul said he would not boast, except in his *infirmities*. He had used exactly the same words in the chapter before (2 Corinthians 11:30) in the middle of a long discourse on all the terrible persecutions he suffered. If you take his "thorn" to mean persecution, chapter 12 makes much more sense.

2 Corinthians 12:7 said the thorn was a messenger of Satan, sent to buffet him. I once heard a minister say, "God doesn't use Satan's messenger service. He has His own messengers (i.e. angels)." We know, therefore, that God did not send the thorn; the verse says it was from Satan.

Paul appeared to be buffeted more than any other person. Wherever he went, that messenger of Satan stirred up trouble, riots occurred, mobs tried to kill him, he was beaten or thrown in prison. He describes all this in 2 Corinthians 11:24-26:

From the Jews five times I received forty stripes minus one. Three times I was beaten with rods; once I was stoned; three times I was shipwrecked; a night and a day I have been in the deep; in journeys often, in perils of waters, in perils of robbers, in perils of my own countrymen, in perils of the Gentiles, in perils in the sea, in perils among false brethren; in weariness and toil, in sleeplessness often, in hunger and thirst, in fastings often, in cold and nakedness—

After this, in verse 30, he says, "If I must boast, I will boast in the things which concern my *infirmity*" then proceeds to talk of more persecution.

So Paul asked Jesus three times that this messenger of Satan might depart from him. There are a couple of vital principles here. After Jesus rose from the dead, nowhere in the New Testament are we told to ask God to do something about the devil. Instead we are told that *we* have been given power and authority over him (Luke 10:19). We are commanded to resist the devil (James 4:7), resist him steadfastly in the faith (1 Peter 5:9), put on the whole armour of God so we can stand against him successfully (Ephesians 6:12-18), quench all his fiery darts with the shield of faith (Ephesians 6:16), cast out devils in the name of Jesus (Mark 16:17), etc.

Secondly, Jesus said that His grace was sufficient. I used to think that sounded a bit like, "There, there, Paul, you'll be alright; My grace is enough for you," but Jesus was talking about a mighty, supernatural power because Paul was able to say in 2 Corinthians 12:10:

> Therefore I take pleasure in infirmities, in reproaches, in needs, in persecutions, in distresses, for Christ's sake. For when I am weak [infirm], then I am strong.

Do you see it? The things he took pleasure in were his weaknesses, the reproaches, needs, persecutions, distresses – all the persecutions he had just talked about in the chapter before. Paul learned to rejoice in these weaknesses/infirmities because he found when he had to rely on the "power of Christ" he received miracles; he was then *really* strong. That is the power of God's grace.

It is also worthy of note that Jesus did not say, "I'm giving you My grace but no, I will not heal you." Those words have been added by many over the years, but they are inconsistent with the rest of the Bible.

Paul Was Sick from Time to Time

That said, Paul does talk about "the infirmity of my flesh" (Galatians 4:13), which seems to indicate sickness. But the Bible does not go on to state that Paul had this sickness because it was not God's will to heal him. Paul, like you and me and everyone else in the world, was attacked by sickness. And obviously, there were times he was not able to fight it off. That is no strike against him.

Healing was always available. Jesus bore every one of Paul's, your and my sicknesses and infirmities on the cross in the same sacrifice where He bore all our sins.

Paul also talked about a friend of his, Trophimus, whom, he said in 2 Timothy 4:20, he had left sick in Miletum. Trophimus, like you and me and Paul, had a bitter enemy who attacked him, and there were times he also needed to battle unbelief to receive the healing Jesus provided.

DON'T DWELL ON THE FEW NEGATIVES

Even though we have been given proof over and over that God wants to heal us, some people seem to want to dwell only on the one or two who were not healed in the Bible. Why? Do they feel God is angry at them or they lack faith? Are they embarrassed when they are told that they could be healed, because they feel it makes them less spiritual to be struggling with sickness? They certainly aren't! Everyone on earth is attacked with and struggles with sickness at times.

I am always saddened when I encounter people who would rather fight to remain sick than accept healing. That is not humility or teachability. Their pride deprives them of a wonderful blessing.

I have said before that I have not always been healed, but I do keep building up my faith to resist the doubts and keep studying healing all the time, and I have been healed over and over again. Many times when a cold, flu, infirmity, or pain tried to come on me, I would quote and meditate on the above truths, and I received healing.

Do you know what? It is absolutely thrilling to be healed! How I love not being sick or in pain. How I love taking the promises and medicine of God's Word and driving away the things the devil tries to put on me. It is so wonderful to be healed after a few hours of resisting sickness and not having to stay in bed or feel terrible for a week.

Does this make me more spiritual? Not in the least. I just happened to have discovered I did not have to be sick, because some precious people brought me the good news, the gospel. And, friend, that is the news I want to bring to you.

I also know what it is to have unbelief overcome me in a situation. But even though that deprived me of a healing or an answer to prayer, down deep inside I still knew beyond a shadow of a doubt that God loved me, and it was then and always will be His will for me to be healed. He made total provision for it. You could never convince me otherwise. For almost forty years, I have searched, marked and studied every verse I could find on healing from the beginning of the Bible to the end in many different versions.

DEATH IS NOT A FAILURE

I feel it is important, just before the end, to add this very important truth. Death is an inevitable fact for all of us. But when Christians die young, or before living what we might consider a "full" life, that is not a failure. They are welcomed into heaven by their Saviour and loving Father, with great joy. The Bible says, "Precious in the sight of the Lord is the death of His saints" (Psalm 116:15).

Many lovely Christians have been attacked with sickness, received prayer, had the laying on of hands, but still struggled with illness and died without having received their manifestation of healing. I believe many of them died believing the best they knew how, which was very pleasing to God.

Not one of us has full revelation on why people die when they do. We do not know all the facts; we do not know what happened behind the scenes in the dark hours during their brave fight against their disease. It certainly does not mean that these Christians are "less than" others who have believed and received healing, or "less than" those who have been healed miraculously by the laying on of hands. In fact, often those who died younger actually lived more loving and fruitful Christian lives than many who have experienced healing.

I have seen sincere Christians who believed in healing, struggling to get rid of doubts, unbelief and the constant attacks on their bodies. I have also seen them become weary of the fight and wish they could go home to heaven. Why not? God would never hold it against them, and neither does He want us to.

He makes it clear in 1 Corinthians 13:1-3 that even if I have faith to move mountains (including sickness-mountains) and have not love, I am nothing.

Yes, healing is available, but I know from experience that sometimes healing can be hard to obtain or maintain. I have had sicknesses from which it took me years to be healed. For other infirmities, I am still "standing" on the Word of God. But, praise the Lord, I have met people who have more developed faith and revelation on healing than I have and what a blessing it is when they are eager to share their faith and help me rather than criticize.

Please do not look down on someone who is struggling with sickness. And especially, do not ever tell bereaved relatives that their loved one died because they did not have enough faith. Oh, what an unloving thing to say. We are told to "weep with those who weep" in Romans 12:15. One of our jobs as Christians is to comfort just as God comforts us. And this comfort is that He loves and doesn't condemn anyone but welcomes His children home to heaven with eager and outstretched arms.

BE ENCOURAGED: GOD WANTS YOU WELL

I want to end with a beautiful verse near the end of the Bible, written by a man many call the "Apostle of Love":

> Beloved, I pray that you may prosper in all things and be in health, just as your soul prospers. 3 John 2

How great is our God's goodness! He is the Lord that heals us! When Jesus was being brutally beaten, when He hung on the cross for us, He was taking not only our sins, but also our sicknesses because He so wanted us always to be healed and live in health!

It is interesting to note in 3 John 2, that our prospering and being in health are in proportion to the prosperity of our souls. I pray that your soul has begun to prosper more as you have read these wonderful truths from our "Lord that heals you." You will be *able* to take the shield of faith and quench *all* the fiery darts of the devil (Ephesians 6:16).

I believe the most important thing a person can do to receive healing is *first of all* to realize it is always God's will for him or her to be healed. If we doubt that foremost fact, it will be very difficult to receive and continue to hold steadfastly onto our faith during pain, bad medical reports, discouragement and especially waiting without seeing any results, for "faith is the evidence of things *not* seen" (Hebrews 11:1). But if we study and meditate on the many verses and passages above, we will be able to "see"

39

ourselves healed and can come to an absolute assurance of God's will to heal us. Then we will be well on our way to receiving healing from any and every disease that attacks our bodies.

Bibliography

[i] Dr. Robert Young, was a Hebrew and Greek Scholar (Old Testament was written in Hebrew, New Testament was written in Greek), and the author of *Hints and Helps to Bible Interpretation.* He says in this book, that in Exodus 15:26, the literal Hebrew reads *"...I will permit to be put upon thee none of these disease which I permitted to be brought upon the Egyptians, for I am the Lord that heals you."* Word Inspire Ministries: "In the Old Testament, Scripture was translated in the causative sense. In most cases, it should have been translated in the permissive sense."
http://www.wordinspire.com/Word%20of%20Life%20Study%20-%20Teacher%27s%20Guide%20-%20Part%201.pdf
[ii] ibid
[iii] Strong's Exhaustive Concordance, H7965
[iv] ibid, G769

If you want to be sure you will go to Heaven after you die, pray this simple prayer:

"Dear Jesus, thank you for dying and taking the full punishment for everyone's sins. I ask and receive your forgiveness for everything I've ever done wrong. I believe in my heart that you are the Son of God and that you rose from the dead. Please make me your own child and come into my life and change it. Thank you so much. I know that I am now born again."

If you prayed this prayer sincerely, the Bible says God makes you a brand "new creature." You actually become a child of God. From now on, he sees you as "righteous," which means your spirit becomes perfect, qualifying you for heaven. He gives you his Holy Spirit to stay with you forever and guide you into all truth. The Holy Spirit will also continually remind you in your heart that you are truly a child of God.

God, your loving Father, longs for you to pray and talk to him intimately. He hears every prayer you pray. He also speaks to you as you read the Bible. Start by reading the New Testament and ask him to reveal its truths to you. He will transform your whole life as you discover his loving will for you.

If you want to know more about this subject, search online for "Prayer of Salvation." There is a wealth of information that will be very helpful and encouraging.

ALSO BY JULENE HODGES SCHROEDER

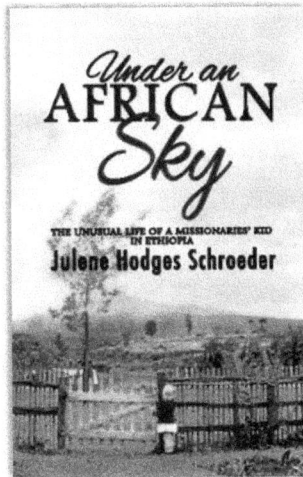

Julene Hodges Schroeder was raised in an Ethiopia that was beginning to emerge from centuries of isolation. When her parents went as missionaries in 1945, they expected to make sacrifices and were tested to the limit. But they never realized how much they would fall in love with that beautiful land and its people, nor how Ethiopia would capture their hearts forever.

Under An African Sky is a story you can read to your children and grandchildren, about a missionaries' kid who lived an unusual life and loved it. Julene writes the story of her childhood with warmth and honesty, sharing its hilarious moments, its lasting friendships and a particular sorrow that is common to missionaries' kids.

You will be warmed to discover how the gospel was introduced in those long-ago days by people who truly did "seek first the kingdom" and how they happily gave up everything for what they considered the greatest adventure!

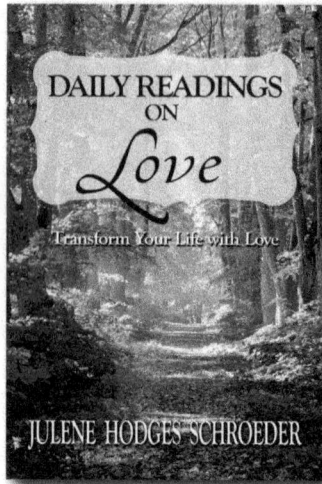

DAILY READINGS
ON
Love

Transform Your Life with Love

JULENE HODGES SCHROEDER

Is your goal in life to find and follow God's heart? But do you find Bible-reading a struggle? Do you wonder where to read, how much and how often?

Julene Hodges Schroeder has created this book to make Bible-reading enjoyable and easy. You can read it by yourself or together with your family. By spending only a few minutes a day, every day, each month, you will find these daily readings will begin to transform your heart, making it more like God's heart.

God's heart is that we love one another. As we learn to walk in love — His kind, merciful, tender, and gracious love — we are doing the most important thing, in God's eyes. In this book, each day's verses speak about a different aspect of love. As you read the daily meditation, over and over, slowly and thoughtfully, these scriptures will implant themselves in your heart.

By meditating and feeding on them, you will find yourself learning how much God loves you. In turn, His love will start working through you in your interactions with all those around you, and you will indeed find yourself becoming more and more like Him.

ABOUT THE AUTHOR

Julene Hodges Schroeder was raised in Ethiopia by missionary parents, who taught her to love God and His Word. For decades, she has been a teacher of the Bible. She longs to see people realize how much God loves them, fall in love with Him and have their lives transformed by knowing the Bible.

Julene lives in Calgary, in the foothills of the beautiful Canadian Rockies. She and her husband have three married children and twelve grandchildren.

www.ingramcontent.com/pod-product-compliance
Lightning Source LLC
LaVergne TN
LVHW011339080426
835513LV00006B/435